CHILDREN'S Fiddling Method

VOLUME 1

By Carol Ann Wheeler

Audio Contents

Disc 1

1	Intro & Tuneup [:47]
2	Lesson #1 [:43]
3	Lesson #2 [1:58]
4	Lesson #3 [:57]
5	Lesson #4 [:56]
6	Lesson #5 [1:21]
7	Lesson #6 [:44]
8	Lesson #7 [:26]
9	Lesson #8 [:51]
10	Lesson #9 [:41]
11	Lesson #10 [:31]
12	Lesson #11 [1:06]
13	Lesson #12 [:51]
14	Lesson #13 [1:28]
15	Lesson #14 [:56]
16	Lesson #15 [:26]
17	Lesson #16 [:55]
18	Lesson #17 [1:05]
19	Lesson #18 [2:25]
20	Lesson #19 [:47]

21	Lesson #20 [:46]
22	Lesson #21 [1:10]
23	Lesson #22 [1:02]
24	Lesson #23 [:31]
25	Lesson #24 [1:21]
26	Lesson #25 [:24]
27	#25 with Drones [:42]
28	Lesson #26 [:50]
29	Lesson #27 [1:30]
30	Lesson #28 [1:08]
31	Lesson #29 [:52]
32	Lesson #30 [1:15]
33	Lesson #31 [:35]
34	Lesson #32 [2:31]
35	Lesson #33 [1:07]
36	Lesson #34 [1:25]
37	Lesson #35 [1:04]
38	Lesson #36 [1:28]
39	Lesson #37 [1:06]
40	Lesson #38 [:59]

41	Lesson #39 [1:42]
42	#39 with Guitar [1:04]
43	Lesson #40 [1:36]
44	Lesson #41 [1:50]
45	Lesson #42 [1:32]

Disc 2

1	Lesson #43 [1:31]
2	Lesson #44 [:23]
3	Lesson #45 [1:04]
4	Lesson #46 [:44]
5	Lesson #47 [1:12]
6	Lesson #48 [:34]
7	Lesson #49 [1:07]
8	#49 with Guitar [:35]
9	Lesson #50 [1:42]
10	Lesson #51 [1:08]
11	Lesson #52 [:37]
12	#52 Licks [:26]
13	Lesson #53 [:55]
	Lesson #54 [:36]

14	Lesson #55 [1:25]
15	Lesson #56 [1:16]
16	Lesson #57 [1:05]
17	Lesson #58 [1:35]
18	Lesson #59 [1:02]
19	Lesson #60 [1:44]
20	Lesson #61 [1:18]
21	Lesson #62 [1:54]
22	Lesson #63 [2:31]
23	Lesson #64 [2:06]
24	Lesson #65 [:43]
25	Lesson #66 [1:49]
26	Lesson #67 [1:22]
27	Lesson #68 [1:53]
28	Lesson #69 [1:00]
29	Lesson #70 [:40]
30	Lesson #71 [1:14]
31	Lesson #72 [1:50]
32	Lesson #73 [:31]

Online Audio & Video

Audio
www.melbay.com/94817EB
Video
dv.melbay.com/94817
You Tube
www.melbay.com/94817V

1 2 3 4 5 6 7 8 9 0

Visit us on the Web at www.melbay.com — E-mail us at email@melbay.com

Contents

About the Author

Carol Ann Wheeler has an extensive background of over 20 years as a violinist, orchestral member, and string teacher for public and private schools. She has always been fascinated by the sound of the fiddle. In 1974 she began to study and learn how to play old-time fiddle. Intrigued by different styles of fiddling, she became a collector and performer of several: old-time, Texas, trick and show fiddling, cross tunes, Canadian, Scottish, and Irish to list some of the styles she enjoys. Since 1974 she has produced five fiddle albums and has been a contest fiddler, judge, and fiddle workshop teacher. She has performed for ten years through Young Audiences of Oregon and Washington, and has traveled and performed in Japan, Canada, and Scotland, as well as the U.S.

Ms. Wheeler taught her own two children (who both became champion fiddlers) how to play fiddle, starting them at very young ages. Her home contains over 200 fiddle-contest trophies, plaques, etc. Through her fiddle workshops, albums, and performances, she has taught and perpetuated fiddle music to thousands. She and her students have won numerous times on the state, regional, and national levels. As announcer Harry Reeves said at the National Fiddle Contest in Weiser, Idaho, "You name it, she's won it!"

Ms. Wheeler is known for being an energetic and enthusiastic performer and for teaching not just notes, but technique and style as well. She is thrilled to be able to reach and perpetuate the art of old-time fiddling to an even larger scope of people through Mel Bay Publications.

Introduction

This book has been designed to start at the very beginning using the simplest of tunes probably already played by the student. Then, common folk songs familiar to the student are used to demonstrate and teach the most basic skills of old-time fiddle. The information is presented one skill at a time in a step-by-step fashion. Students can progress at their own pace, and by the middle of the book they are learning authentic old-time fiddle tunes. Basic arrangements are offered, enabling the very young to play, while several alternate variations on a more advanced skill level are also presented so that more advanced fiddlers may be challenged. Younger students may return at a future time and *add* the advanced versions as they "grow into" them. Students are continually encouraged to strive for quality in their playing, and are assisted to feel good about themselves and their own personal progress.

This method, while designed for children, can also be utilized by adult fiddle students, as well as by violin and fiddle teachers as an excellent teacher's aid.

Cassette Tape

Equally important to the fiddle student is the *listening tape,* where tunes and music examples are played *slowly* and up to tempo by champion fiddler/master teacher Carol Ann Wheeler, so that at completion of this volume the budding fiddler is not simply *playing the notes* of a fiddle tune, but hopefully playing with a *true* "fiddle style." A solid foundation and understanding of *how to play the fiddle* are laid and the student is ready to progress to more difficult tunes not only in this series, but also those offered in the wealth of fiddle-tune collections from Mel Bay Publications.

Getting Started

Today is a very exciting, special day! Today you begin learning to play the *fiddle!* Playing fiddle is a little different from violin. You will play old-time fiddle tunes and folk songs from our past. Some of the songs have roots from other countries, as our forefathers, the pioneers, often came from other lands like Ireland and Scotland. Other tunes were born right in America. Each of the tunes is like a little piece of history.

In fiddling, you will use techniques different from those in the violin world. In fiddling, you will be allowed more freedom to change the tunes and play them *your* way and be creative. That's where the saying "fiddling around" comes from. Being able to play both violin and fiddle is fun!

Let's Get Started Now!

For many of you, TWINKLE, TWINKLE LITTLE STAR may have been your first tune. Just to make sure, here's a review (Arrangement #1):

Lesson #1: Twinkle, Twinkle Little Star (Basic Tune)

Lesson #2: Shuffle Bowing

Now let's take TWINKLE and use it to learn some fiddle techniques and skills that you will use all of your fiddling life! Using the *same* notes, we'll simply change the rhythm. If you played Suzuki violin, your violin teacher may have called this rhythm by names like "Hop, Bun-ny! Hop, Bun-ny!" or "*Long*, Short, Short, *Long*, Short, Short" (referring to the length of the notes). In the fiddle world it is called "shuffle bowing." I also call it "hoedown rhythm" and "fiddle rhythm" because it is used *a lot* in fiddle hoedowns. Hoedowns or breakdowns are those fast tunes that fiddlers are known for playing.

Music Ex. 1

Try this rhythm on your A string. Notice that one time you use a *down* bow on the long note, then an *up* bow.

Long-short-short

Fiddlers often call a little group of notes a "lick." Play this lick on all four open strings.

Ex. 2

Now try the lick on pairs of open strings. I like to think "top pair" (A and E), "middle pair," etc. See if you can play accenting *on* the beat and also accenting on the *off beat*.

Ex. 3

Accent *on* the beat.

Accent on the *off* beat.

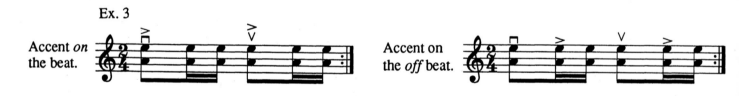

And you'll want to play it on all three pairs of strings, as you'll use all three pairs when you play fiddle.

Ex. 4

Accent *on* the beat.

Accent on the *off* beat.

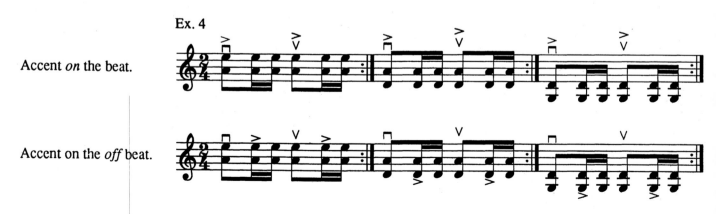

Lesson #3: Twinkle with Shuffle Bowing

Now let's play TWINKLE using shuffle bowing or fiddle rhythm. First we'll play on *single* strings.

Twinkle with Hoedown Rhythm
Arrangement #2

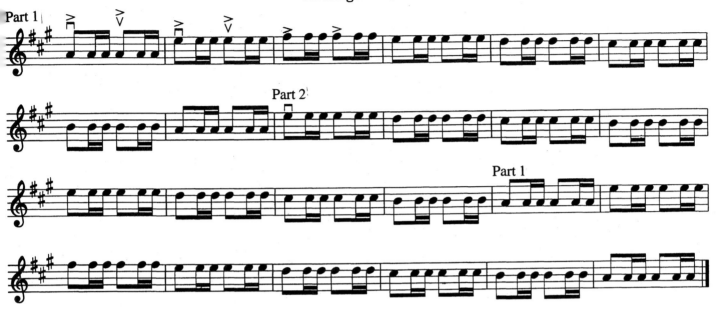

Lesson #4: Twinkle on Double Strings

When you feel comfortable with single strings, then we can add playing on *two strings* at the same time. When you are on the A string, simply let your bow also play on the E string, and when you are fingering on the E string, let your bow play on the A string. This is actually pretty simple, but when you see it written out in music, it can appear busy and complicated. Don't let this worry you. You are simply playing the *whole* tune (after the opening A) on *two* strings.

Here's what it looks like:

Twinkle with Hoedown Rhythm on Two Strings
Arrangement #3

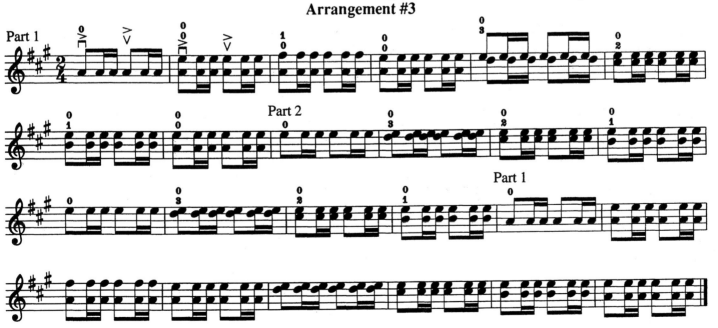

Lesson #5: The Slide

When you are able to play TWINKLE on two strings at the same time, then we are ready to start the really exciting and fun part: *adding the fiddle flavor* or *fiddle style!* I think this is where the tune really starts to *sound* like fiddling (instead of violin). So let's learn some fiddle techniques.

First the slide. Fiddlers will slide into certain notes. Certainly not all notes, but their playing is sprinkled with slides. Some slides are fast, some are slower. Listening to your tape will help you with the speed of slides.

To make a slide, place your finger about ½ inch below (called a "half step" in violin) the note and slide *up* to the note. *Do not slide past the note.*

I use a curved arrow ⌣ pointing *up* over the notes that I like to slide into.

Ex. 1: Sliding the First Finger on the E String. Place your first finger ½ inch (a half step) below F♯ (*on* F♮) and *slide it up*…to F♯. Practice your first-finger slides on the E string now.

Of course, first-finger slides can be played on any of your four strings. Now let's practice them on the other three strings.

We will also be using slides with our *second* finger on the A string, the note C♯. You will place your finger approximately ½ inch below C♯ on the note C♮ and slide it *up* to the note C♯.

Again, it is good for us to practice second-finger slides on all four strings.

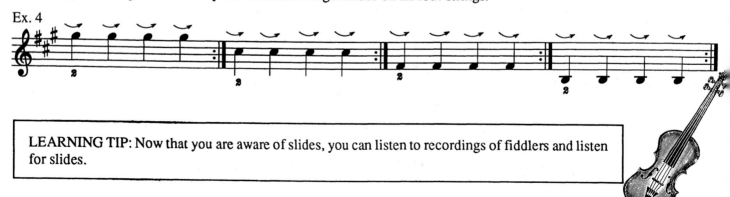

LEARNING TIP: Now that you are aware of slides, you can listen to recordings of fiddlers and listen for slides.

Lesson #6: Hoedown Introduction

Now our TWINKLE needs an *introduction*. Fiddlers will frequently play little introductions (extra shuffles) before beginning hoedowns. The minute an audience hears these exciting fast notes, their ears immediately perk up and their feet begin tapping! The introduction tells the guitar (and other back-up players or dancers), "Hey! Here we go!" Introductions are always played in the *key of the tune*, and they set the tempo for the entire tune.

I have heard fiddlers call their introductions by "potatoes." Byron Berline told me he made that nickname up years ago.

When I say, "OK, I'll give you four potatoes..." I might play this:

4-potatoes introduction

Or I might play this:

It depends on whether the tune starts *on* the *down* beat, or on a "pick-up" note. Sometimes I just like a long drag here (a "po" instead of "po-ta-to"), as it gives me a chance to think.

Lesson #7: Hoedown Endings (Tags and Shaves)

Now, with the addition of an *ending*, our TWINKLE, TWINKLE LITTLE STAR (Hoedown Style) will have all the parts for making it into "fiddle style"! I call an ending a "shave," as it comes from that old phrase we have all chanted, "Shave and a haircut, two bits!"

Since this is our very first tune, we'll keep it simple for now and use open strings.

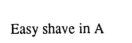

Bowing: Play TWINKLE around the middle of the bow if you are playing slowly or at a medium speed. The *faster* you play, the *more of the upper half of the bow* you use.

When you get to the last two notes, play them *at the frog* of the bow (down by your hand).

Now we have all of our information — the tricks that change TWINKLE from just plain notes into a fiddle tune: shuffle bowing, double strings, slides, a fiddler's intro, and a fiddler's ending. Let's put them all together. Of course, there will be a lot to think about. Pick one trick and work on it, then pick another until you have learned them all. Practice them by yourself, listen to me play on the tape, then your final goal will be to play *along with me* on the tape. Wearing earphones for part of your practice time when you are playing along with me is a good learning technique.

Lesson #8: Twinkle, Twinkle Little Star (Fiddle Style)

Arrangement #4

Chords: Notice that the chords appear in this, our final arrangement of TWINKLE, TWINKLE LITTLE STAR, in case you wish to have piano or guitar accompaniment. Back-up chords will appear in all final arrangements of the tunes throughout this book. Once you learn a tune, playing with accompaniment is the really fun part.

Lesson #9: Double E's (An Advanced Technique)

Optional variation: Here's a technique that you can add when you feel ready for a new challenge. It's something that fiddlers use a lot, and I just love this sound. I call it a "double E" or "drone E's." You will, in addition to playing your open E string, play four fingers down on the A string (creating the note E...), creating *double E's*. If you use a "slide" on the fourth finger, it makes a great sound against the open E string.

You can use the *double E's* in measure 9 and measure 13.

You'll want to learn this technique as soon as you are able, as it is a really wonderful skill not used in the violin world but very important in the fiddle world.

Practicing "drones" on all pairs of your strings will help prepare you for other tunes.

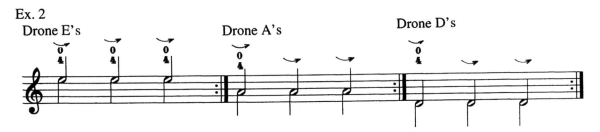

Lesson #10: The A Scale

Our first tune, TWINKLE, TWINKLE LITTLE STAR, was in the key of A. Our second tune, FRENCH FOLK SONG, is also in the key of A. Fiddlers play a lot in the key of A. They like this key because it allows the fiddler to use lots of open strings in the fiddle tunes.

The key of A has *three* sharps (♯). Notice the three "tic tac toe" signs on each line of music? A sharp raises a note *up* a half step, which is about ½ inch higher. When you play violin, it is important to know and understand *what* key you are playing in. As a fiddler, it is also important to know and understand your keys. By knowing the key, you know *where* to place your fingers. For example, in the A scale below you will want to use a *high* second finger on the A and E strings.... Why? Because you are in the key of A, and that is where the half steps fall.

Play through this one-octave *A scale:*

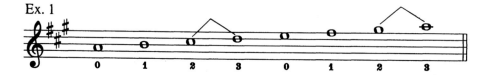

In the word "octave," "oct" means "eight" and "tave" means "step." Your scale has eight steps!

Notice the slanted (∧) mark? This shows you where the half steps are. When you have a half step, your fingers will be *right next* to each other and probably touch. In major scales the half steps always fall between the *same* steps in the scale — the third and fourth notes and the seventh and eighth notes.

It's good to know what key you are in so you can tell your back-up and other people who you might be jamming with, so that they can play along with you.

Parts of scales and even *whole* scales can occur in fiddle tunes, so the better you know your scales the better you can play your tunes.

Can you find the A scale in the first eight measures of FRENCH FOLK SONG? And look! There's another A scale in the last four measures!

Lesson #11: French Folk Song (Basic Tune)

Fiddlers are probably most thought of as playing fast, but the fact is they can and do play slow lovely tunes, also. Let's try a slower tune now, a *waltz*. A waltz is a type of dance. Waltzes are always in 3/4 meter. That means three beats to a measure. (Count "**One**, two, three, **One**, two, three.")

If you studied the Suzuki method of violin, you probably played FRENCH FOLK SONG. We'll add some fiddle techniques and call it FRENCH WALTZ. Fiddlers play waltzes for dancing and for their own and others' listening enjoyment. When you play in American or Canadian fiddle contests, you will need to play a waltz as part of your contest set.

Let's first review the basic tune.

French Folk Song
Arrangement #1

Lesson #12: French Waltz
Arrangement #2

Now let's "fiddle" FRENCH FOLK SONG into a waltz! In the violin world, one rarely changes what is written in the music, but that's just one more difference from the fiddle world. Here are a few changes in the rhythm and a couple of notes that I might personally play. Remember, every fiddler has his or her own way, most likely different from mine, to fiddle any tune. Of course, we would never change *how many beats are in a measure,* only what happens *within the measure.*

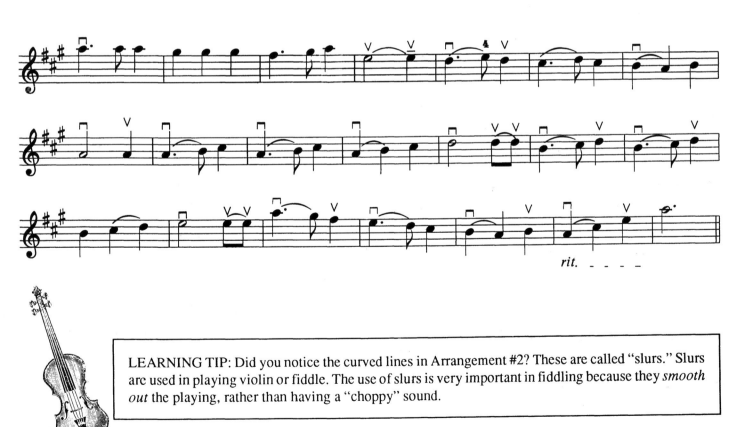

LEARNING TIP: Did you notice the curved lines in Arrangement #2? These are called "slurs." Slurs are used in playing violin or fiddle. The use of slurs is very important in fiddling because they *smooth out* the playing, rather than having a "choppy" sound.

Did you notice that I added some slurs to the bowing? The way a fiddler bows is *very important* to that fiddler's individual style. The more you want to capture a certain fiddler's sound or style, the more important it is that you copy his or her bowing.

Lesson #13: More New Ornaments (Flicks and Roll-Ups)

In TWINKLE we used slides to decorate. Now we are going to learn some more new fiddle techniques — "flicks"! Fiddlers will often decorate some of the notes with a little quick flick of the finger, so I like to call them "flicks." In the violin world, they are called "grace notes." Ex. 1: When there is a group of notes (two or more), then I call them "roll-ups." They are like a quick little scale. Ex 3: Look in measure 17 of Lesson #14 and you'll see an example of a roll-up.

To prepare ourselves for adding ornaments to FRENCH WALTZ, let's play some flicks and roll-ups. First-finger flick = flick the note *above*.

Ex. 1. You can flick from *above*.

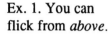 

To *decorate* the first finger, play the first finger, flick the note above, and then come *right back* to the first finger.

Ex. 2. You can flick from *below*.

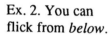 

Decorating third finger with flick from *below*.

Ex. 3. Roll-Ups

Practice roll-ups on all strings.

Decorating third finger with a roll-up.

LEARNING TIP: Strive for a feeling of *relaxation* in the fingers of your left hand when playing flicks and roll-ups.

Lesson #14: French Waltz with Ornaments
Arrangement #3

When you feel comfortable with the ornaments and changing the rhythm of some of the notes, then we are ready for the really fun part — adding them to our waltz! I think it would be a good idea to *first* listen to me playing FRENCH WALTZ on your tape. *Listening will help you understand* the sound you are trying to make. Listening really helps you to capture the fiddle style.

I have written out for you here all of the ornaments I play in FRENCH WALTZ. It is probably better for you to try adding *one* ornament at a time, *not* all of them at once. Don't feel you have to do them all now. You can add them over a period of time at your own pace. That's how I learned to play fiddle…a little at a time.

LEARNING TIP: At measures 4, 8, and 16, I have used those double E's and double A's that I mentioned in TWINKLE. I think these will be the hardest ornaments for you, especially if you are new to violin or haven't developed your fourth finger yet. If you want, it's fine to leave them out for now. Continue to listen to the wonderful fiddle sound of double E's, then try putting them in later after you have worked on them.

Lesson #15: Waltz Endings

The endings of tunes offer the fiddler a chance for creativity. In measure 20 of Arrangement #3, I chose to end with an upward movement. The possibilities for endings are endless! Here's one with a downward movement (Ex. 1):

15

"Fat-finger" technique: Notice in Ex. 2 that I have a double stop (two different notes on two different strings) on the G and D strings. I nickname this a "fat-finger 1" ("f.f."), meaning that your first finger is placed on *two* strings at the same time. Usually when you play violin or fiddle you want your fingers on their tips, but it may be necessary in this case to place your finger *more flat,* that is, more on the fleshy part rather than its tip, so that it is *fat enough* to play on two strings at the same time.

As you listen to your tape, notice how I slow down at the end of the waltz. It gives a nice feeling of finality.

Again, do not feel that you have to do every single decoration that I do. Play whatever you can do well. Remember your goal is *not* necessarily to play fancy or complicated, but *to play well.* As you listen to other fiddlers, you will hear other variations you can add to make up your own arrangement. The freedom to be creative in fiddling is one of the aspects I love. It is one of the features that makes it different from the violin world.

Lesson #16: Go Tell Aunt Rhody (Basic Tune)
Arrangement #1

GO TELL AUNT RHODY is another tune often played in the violin world that also makes a great fiddle tune. Let's review the basic tune first, concentrating on the notes.

Lesson #17: Something New in the Introduction (Chops)

Before we "fiddle" GO TELL AUNT RHODY, let's work on our *intro* and *ending tag.*

This time, in our introduction we'll add two quick notes I call "chops" *just before* the "potatoes." Chops are just part of my (and a lot of fiddlers') personal style. Chops are played with *down* bows at the *frog of the bow.* Potatoes are played in the *middle* of the bow (depending on the speed of the tune) to the *upper half* of your bow. So here's an important secret: You do your two chops at the frog, then on your *first* "po" you "travel" (move your bow fast!) to the upper half and finish the "ta-to" in that part of the bow. So many fiddlers think that the *fingers* are the important thing in fiddling, but the truth is the bow is *just as important.*

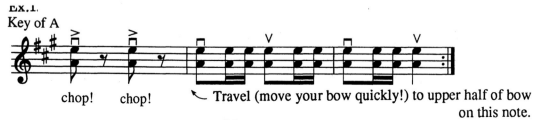

16

Play our introduction on the other pairs of strings, and you change keys!

Ex.2
Key of D

Ex.3
Key of G

Lesson #18: New Fiddler's Tag

Let's learn an authentic fiddler's tag, the one most frequently played. This is the tag that most of the others come from:

First, the notes. Play this tag 30 to 50 times daily until your fingers fly through the notes without your brain needing to *tell* them where to go.

Alternate Bowing Pattern

After you can play the notes with single bowing as in Ex. 1, add the slurs as in Ex. 2. I call this pattern of bowing (two notes slurred, two notes alone…two together, two alone) *the alternate bowing pattern*. It's a very important style of bowing commonly used by fiddlers. It's important to remember to play with single bowing (one note = one bow) if you wish to have a more choppy sound, and to use slurs or the alternate bowing pattern if you want a *smoother* sound.

Ex. 2. Adding *the alternate bowing* pattern to *smooth out* your fiddling.

Now a nice variation is to take the two eighth notes and make them into sixteenths, giving it a more complicated and busier sound.

Ex. 3   Ex. 4

Alternate bowing pattern.

And we can add this new shave to our old shave from TWINKLE, and we'll call it a "double shave" (Ex. 5).

Double Shave

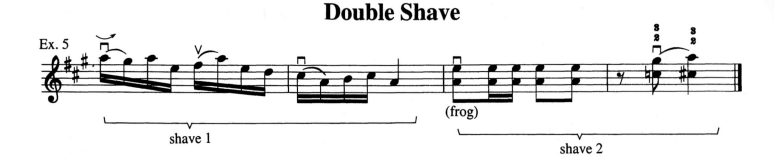

For the last note you might choose to end on a high note as above in Ex. 5. If you want easy notes to play, you could keep them open-string notes (such as we played in TWINKLE) as in Ex. 6. My favorite is "going down in the basement" and playing a fat-finger 1 on the G and D strings as in Ex. 7. To play this chord, you first play a *low* 1 on the G and D strings, then slide into a regular first finger.

You can learn all of these endings for your collection, or just work on *one* for now.

Lesson #19: Adding Shuffle Bowing to Aunt Rhody
Arrangement #2

When you feel comfortable with the notes in AUNT RHODY, then we'll begin to "fiddle" it, just as in TWINKLE, by adding *shuffle bowing*.

Lesson #20: Playing Aunt Rhody on Double Strings
Arrangement #3

When we add double strings to the music, it begins to appear complicated, but it is easier when you realize you are simply playing *the whole tune* on your A and E (your upper pair) strings!

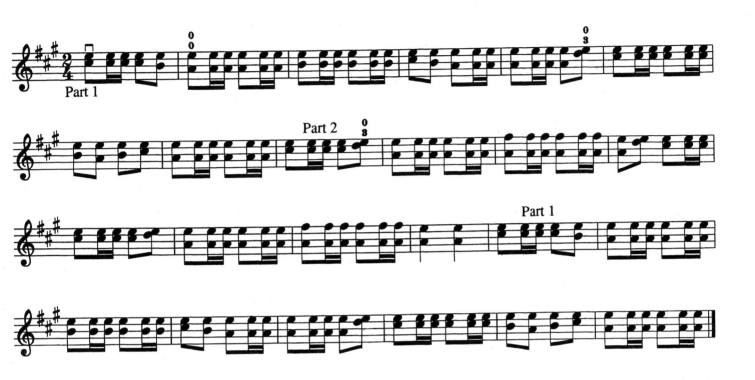

Lesson #21: Go Tell Aunt Rhody (Complete Fiddle Style)

Over a period of time, at your own pace, you can add the remaining fiddling techniques we have already learned in the first two tunes. *Take your time!* Remember to aim for *quality*. As you accomplish one skill, reward yourself by adding another.

Shuffle Bowing • Double Strings • Slides • Flicks • Double E's

Optional advanced technique: You could play double E's in measures 10, 14, and 16, or add this advanced skill at a later date.

Listen to your tape — play along with it!

Go Tell Aunt Rhody (Fiddle Style)
Arrangement #4

AUNT RHODY, when written out, can look rather busy with all of the notes. Just remember when you are fingering on the A string, let your bow also play on the E string. And when you are fingering on the E string, let the open A string sound.

You can play GO TELL AUNT RHODY fast for a hoedown, or you could slow it down and play it as a *two-step*. A two-step could be used as the third tune (tune of choice) in a standard American fiddle contest.

If you decide to play it as a two-step, do not use the hoedown introduction or the hoedown ending (shave). Use only the two chops to start, and only a long note (drag) to end (Ex. 1).

Lesson #22: The Key of G

In preparation for our next tune, we'll play a G scale. We'll play it on the G and D strings, then up the A and E strings. There will actually be two scales, one on top of the other. This is called a "two-octave scale."

Ex. 1

Then play the G scale with the alternate bowing pattern.

Ex. 2

> What does playing in the key of G *mean* to a fiddler?
>
> Answer: That you have a *high* 2 on the G and D strings, but a *low* 2 on the A and E strings. *And* all of your *3's* are in the same place, with none of them being a *high* 3.
>
> *Why?* Because when you start the scale on the note G, that is where the half steps fall.

Lesson #23: Red River Valley (Two-Step Basic Tune)

Our first three tunes were in the key of A, a very popular key for fiddle tunes. Now let's try the key of G in an old folk song, a two-step that our forefathers used to sing and dance to, RED RIVER VALLEY.

First here's the "bare bones" tune:

Red River Valley (Two-Step)
Arrangement #1

Key of G

Lesson #24: Red River Valley with Ornaments
Arrangement #2

Now, with the addition of a few slides and ornaments, we can turn it into a very lovely fiddle tune, one you could use to entertain an audience. Or you might play it as a tune of choice in a fiddle contest, or you could play it at a dance.

Did you notice something new in measure 9 — the curved arrow pointing in a *downward* direction? I use this to indicate a slide *down from* a note, a kind of "melting out of" effect I really enjoy using. (See Ex. 1.)

Practice sliding *up to* the note B and then *down*, out of the note B until you can play it smoothly.

Optional variations and ornaments: Here are some additional ideas you can try when you feel ready to experiment. Try them all to find the ones you like best.

In Ex. 3 is a roll-up which I like to add sometimes in measure 8.

Lesson #25: Red River Valley with Double Strings

The use of double stops, or "drone strings" : Adding some drone strings can add a fuller, richer sound. You could take the approach of just adding them occasionally by sprinkling them here and there, as in Ex. 1 and Ex. 2.

Or, if you like a heavier sound, you could use them throughout the whole tune as in Arrangement #3.

Notice, however, that in measure 11 I have used a *real* double stop (with a first finger on the D string and a second finger on the A string) as I did not like the sound of the open D string in this measure. I put them in parentheses to indicate they are optional, so if they are too hard for you at this time, leave them out.

Red River Valley with Drones
Arrangement #3

Lesson #26: Endings for Red River Valley

About endings: You can do your own thing on your ending for RED RIVER VALLEY. You could keep it very simple as above, or here are four different endings for you to try. Perhaps you have some ideas for endings of your own.

Ex. 1. Keeping it simple.

Ex. 2. Using a downward G-scale movement.

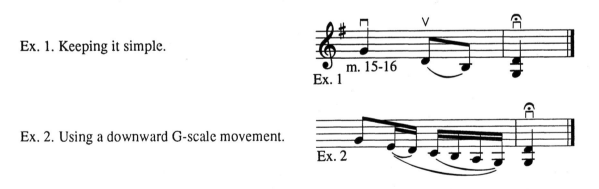

Ex. 3: Alternate Last Note for Ex. 2 for Advanced Students. In this double stop, treat your second and third fingers as a team (they are right next to each other and move together).

Perhaps you are in the mood to end with an upward movement like Ex. 4.

Slightly more complicated is the addition of the double stop, which is a very characteristic fiddle sound.

Lesson #27: Home on the Range (Waltz)

Since you are now more familiar with "how-to-fiddle" techniques, I'll write out the whole tune including some ornaments, etc. You can leave them out for a while and just stick with the basic tune until you feel more confident with the notes, then begin adding ornaments a few at a time. As you learn one "fiddlely-diddlely" as I call them, reward yourself by tackling another decoration of your choice!

You are probably already familiar with this old folk song which can also be played as a very pretty waltz. There are a few double stops which I put in parentheses that you can add when you feel ready.

Home on the Range (Waltz)
Arrangement #1

Playing the waltz above is just fine. However, if you'd like to explore a few of the additional fiddling ideas that you could also play in this waltz, here are a few. It would be good for you to try them all. It's possible you might use them somewhere else in other tunes.

Lesson #28: Home on the Range (Optional Variations)

In measure 7 we have the chance to use that old favorite of fiddlers, double A's (use of the fourth finger with the *open* string above). Sliding *into* the fourth finger, then decorating it with a first-finger flick on the open A *while still holding down* the fourth finger really sounds great (Ex. 1)!

Here's another way to fiddle measure 15 (Ex. 2).

At measure 17 we could use my old favorite, the roll-up, *instead* of sliding into your third finger (the note D) (Ex. 3).

You could also use a roll-up in measure 1.

The long note in measure 19 could be fiddled sometimes like this for variety (Ex. 4).

Or the same spot might be fiddled this way (Ex. 5).

Fiddlers often call a little group of notes a "lick." Here's a lick I think sounds especially good fiddled in measure 23 (Ex. 6). Play the little downward scale *while* your bow *also* plays the open A.

I feel you will want to play through HOME ON THE RANGE twice. When you repeat it, you could put in some of the alternate variations. You *do not* have to play the tune exactly the same each time. It's fine and *fun* to "mix your licks" and do the tune differently every time you play it. You'll probably find that you enjoy some licks better than others, so you'll play those more often.

Now, let's turn our attention to the ending. Here are five possibilities for you to try. Which ones do you like? Can you make up your own ending?

Lesson #29: Optional/Different Endings for Home on the Range

Ex. 1 is a very typical waltz ending used by fiddlers. Notice that the last note is G. In fiddle tunes, the last note is usually the *key* of the tune.

m. 31
Ex. 1

HOME ON THE RANGE can be played *slowly* in a beautiful lyrical style. It could also be played more briskly in a more danceable style called "old timey." In that case, you would use very little ritard (slowing down) at the end and keep it more perky. This style of ending would be more in character (Ex. 2).

m. 31
Ex. 2

The last note could be a bit more challenging by playing a B on the G string (two fingers on the G) (Ex. 3).

m. 31
Ex. 3

The "3"s above the notes in Ex. 4 do not refer to fingering but indicate *triplets*. The use of triplets is very common in fiddle tunes. I use them in the ending. Put a little emphasis on the *first* of each of the triplet groups to accentuate them.

Notice how all of my last notes are played with a *down bow* (⊓)? Be sure to plan ahead for this last note so that you have a nice big *whole bow* for them (Ex. 4).

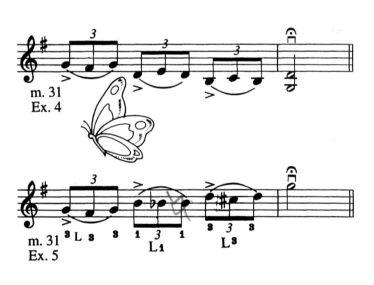

m. 31
Ex. 4

Again, if you like the sound of the higher notes, you might choose to play an ending using an upward movement (Ex. 5).

m. 31
Ex. 5

Lesson #30: Home on the Range with More Advanced Ornaments

Listen to your tape to hear more advanced ornaments used in HOME ON THE RANGE. Here it is written out. Remember that these are only some of the possibilities. You can choose any of them or mix them up according to your personal taste. It's OK *not* to play it exactly the same every time. As a matter of fact, I would play this waltz using certain ornaments on one day, and the next day change them around!

Home on the Range (Waltz) with More Advanced Ornaments
Arrangement #2

LEARNING TIP: When you see double stops with a " >," this is to remind you that these fingers are close to each other, probably touching.

#31: A New Hoedown (She'll Be Comin' Round the Mountain)

an old folk song that all of us have had fun singing. Music was a very important part of the lives of ...ie pioneers because it was used for entertainment. Remember this was a time when there were no TVs, no planes or cars, no radios or tape recorders. Fiddlers supplied the music for many of the dances. SHE'LL BE COMIN' ROUND THE MOUNTAIN makes a great hoedown. Hoedowns, breakdowns, and reels are the faster tunes played at square dances.

First, let's play the basic tune just as you might sing it.

She'll Be Comin' Round the Mountain (Basic Tune)
Arrangement #1

Lesson #32: Intros and Endings for Comin' Round the Mountain

Now we're ready to "fiddle" it! First we'll need our introduction. You remember hoedown rhythm…"potatoes." This introduction tells our back-up or the dancers, "Hey! Here we go — this rhythm!" Since we are now in the key of G, we have several to choose from. Try them all to see and *feel* which intro you like.

Intro #1. This one is the easiest and is just fine.

Intro #2. If you like a *low* sound, you might choose this one on the G and D strings.

Intro #3. Here are the *same* notes but in the middle register of the fiddle. Personally, I enjoy this one because I can slide so easily with the first finger.

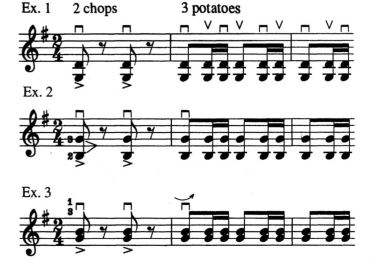

And we'll need our ending tag ("Shave and a Haircut").

Ending #1. This one is very easy, using the shave rhythm with plain open string.

Ex. 4

Ending #2. We can use the popular shave that we learned for RHODY. Since we are now in the key of G, we just move it over two sets of strings to the G and D strings, and use the *same* fingers!

Ex. 5

Ending #3: Single Shave. We can have a *single* shave or a double shave. Sometimes I like to have a plain old long drag (just a long note) on the end.

Ex. 6

Ending #4: Double Shave. Or you can get fancier if that is your style or mood.

Ex. 7

Ex. 8. You can take an ending that you like and, simply by *changing the rhythm* a little, give it variety. For example, let's take Ending #1 and change the rhythm. Here are three different ways to play it.

Ex. 8a

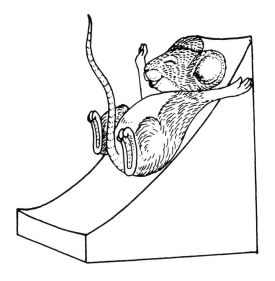

Ex. 8b

Ex. 8c

Let's add our introduction and ending tag to SHE'LL BE COMIN' ROUND THE MOUNTAIN, plus some hoedown rhythm, a couple of slides and drones, and our tune is complete!

She'll Be Comin' Round the Mountain
Arrangement #2

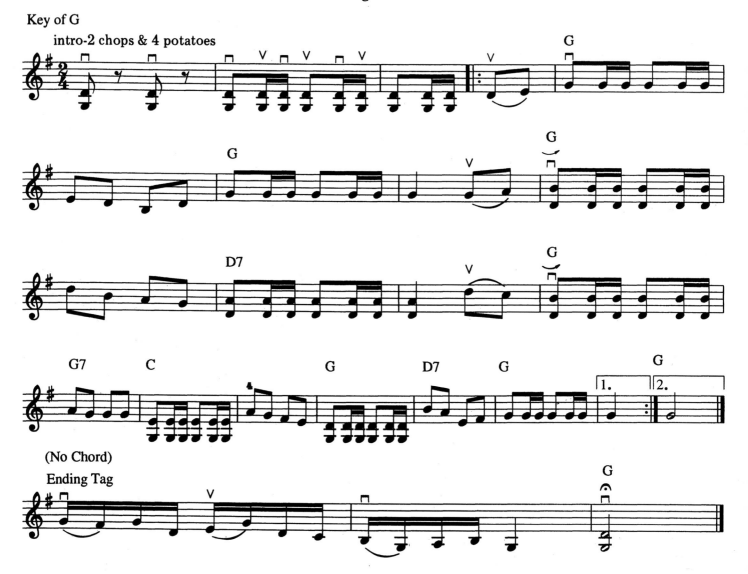

Lesson #34: Novelty or Trick Fiddling

Fiddlers will play tunes with special novelty features to entertain themselves or others. Sometimes they will have tunes for "trick fiddle" contests. Our next tune, POP! GOES THE WEASEL, is a great starter novelty tune.

In the music you will see a "+" over a couple of open E strings. The "+" indicates *left-hand* pizzicato. Use the *third* finger of your left hand to pull or pluck the E string. This is how the fiddler imitates the "Pop!" in POP! GOES THE WEASEL.

If you were short of tunes and made the cut to the second round of a fiddle contest, you could use POP! GOES THE WEASEL as a *tune of choice* (two-step). In a standard American fiddle contest, the fiddler plays three tunes, first a hoedown, second a waltz, then the tune of choice (something *other than* a hoedown or waltz). Other types of tunes used are rags, jigs, polkas, blues, and schottisches.

It is very important that you understand that the use of pizzicato in many contests is considered trick fiddling. It is fine for special trick contests but is not allowed in regular contests. In that case, you could substitute the pizzicato by simply leaving it out and using your bow to play the note E.

Pop! Goes the Weasel (Novelty Tune)
Arrangement #1

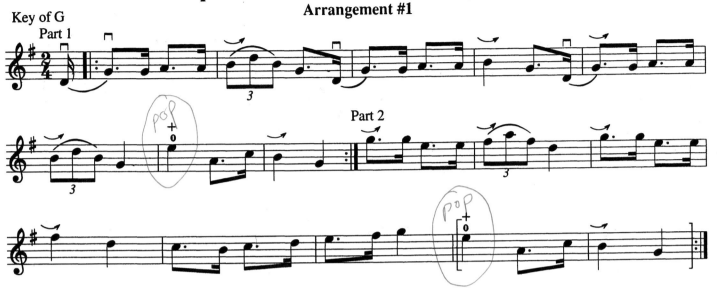

Lesson #35: Pop! Goes the Weasel with Roll-Ups

Playing the above basic arrangement of POP! GOES THE WEASEL would be fine. If you wish to dress it up a bit, here it is with a few roll-ups sprinkled in, as well as a few subtle variations. You could combine *both* arrangements.

You could play through the tune two or three times. When you are ready to end the tune, I like to repeat the last *two measures* as an ending tag. Make a big deal of it, as it gives a feeling of polish and a solid ending. You can hear this solid-ending feel on your tape.

Pop! Goes the Weasel
Arrangement #2

31

Lesson #36: Southwind (Waltz Basic Tune)

Here's a very beautiful lyrical waltz that comes from a very old traditional Irish air. Let's get comfortable with the basic notes before we begin to "fiddle" it.

Southwind (Waltz Basic Tune)
Arrangement #1

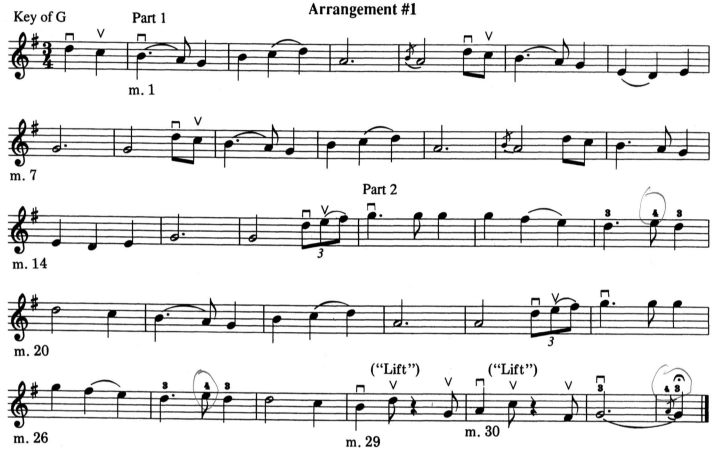

LEARNING TIP: As you listen to SOUTHWIND on your tape, notice the "light touch" at measures 29 and 30. To get this sound, do not leave your bow *on* the string, but "lift" your bow off the string.

Lesson #37: Southwind with Ornaments

You have already been introduced to all of the ornaments that I will play in the next arrangement of SOUTHWIND. Listen to your tape to hear how I play them. Notice that I use *up* slides as well as *down* slides.

Also note that in measures 16 and 24 triplets occur. The "3" indicates a triplet (three notes squeezed into the same amount of time used for *two* notes).

I usually think of waltzes as falling into two categories: the slow *lyrical* (expressive, big-tone) waltz and those *old-timey* waltzes (more up tempo, bouncy, with a danceable beat). I like SOUTHWIND played in a lyrical style, but you could also play it with a peppy old-timey beat. Try it both ways!

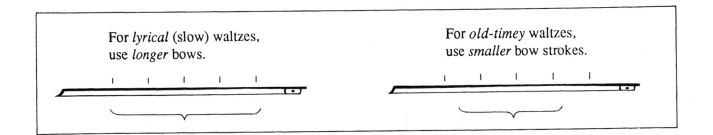

For *lyrical* (slow) waltzes, use *longer* bows.

For *old-timey* waltzes, use *smaller* bow strokes.

Southwind (Waltz) with Ornaments
Arrangement #2

REMINDER: Please do not feel you must play *all* of the ornaments in SOUTHWIND that I play. First choose an ornament or two that you like the sound of and are easy for you. Then, over a period of time, add more ornaments as you feel ready for a challenge. It took me a *long* time to learn these ornaments. I can help you learn them faster than I did, but enjoy yourself! Take your time and go for *quality of sound*. I feel it is much better to do just a few ornaments and *play them well* (clean and clear) than to use too many and play them messy.

Lesson #38: The Key of D

As we play a one-octave D scale, notice that we *begin* and *end* the scale on the note D, the *name* of the scale. Again, our fingers are close together (touching) between the third and fourth notes and seventh and eighth notes of the scale, as that is where the half steps always fall in major scales. Notice also that there are *two* sharps (♯) now.

Ex. 1

Since we'll be using the rest of the notes in the key of D that occur *before* and *after* this written D scale, it would be good for us to play through them, also.

Ex. 2

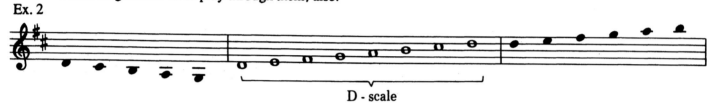

D - scale

So far we have played through *three* keys in this book — G, D, and A. Here's a little trick to help you memorize how many sharps are in each key...your fiddle will help tell you! It has the answers right on its front! Consider your G string as the *first* string:

Our *first* string, the G string...
*The key of G has **one** sharp.*

Our *second* string, the D string...
*The key of D has **two** sharps.*

Our *third* string, the A string...
*The key of A has **three** sharps.*

Our *fourth* string, the E string...
*The key of E has **four** sharps.*

Key of G

Key of D

Key of A

Key of E

LEARNING TIP: To a fiddler, being in the key of D means a *low* 2 on the E string, but a *high* 2 on *all* the other strings.

Lesson #39: Peek-A-B

If you find that you love playing fiddle, you will want to think ab
Each organization has groups of tunes that everyone knows and
is played frequently in my home state's organization, the Orego
pioneers came to America from many different countries: Irela
probably has Swedish roots.

Now that you feel more at home with fiddling, I'll give you the enti
play it. If you wish, you could first learn just the notes, then add the o
have to play them all.

PEEK-A-BOO is one of those *old-timey* danceable waltzes. Play with
measure. I call this "playing with a fat 1"...**One**-two-three, **One**-two-

Peek-A-Boo (Waltz)

Ex. 1 Optional Endings

Ex. 2

35

...n #40: Liberty (Hoedown)

...nes are old — 50, 100, 200 years old! If you are going to be a fiddler, you'll want
... your collection. Fiddlers all over America play it. In fact, when I was performing in
... player there invited me to play it with him. When you play these old tunes, you feel you
...ack into our history and helping to preserve it. LIBERTY was written in 1776 when the U.S.
...ependence from England, and fiddlers have been playing it for over 200 years.

...let's play a simplified arrangement.

Liberty (Simplified Arrangement)
Arrangement #1

LEARNING TIP: Did you notice that groups of notes (finger patterns) are sometimes *repeated?* When
I learn a tune, I use the ideas of patterns to help me. Notice the special lines to indicate patterns I see:
〜〜〜〜〜〜〜〜〜〜〜〜〜〜〜   and - - - - - - - - - - - - - - - - - -

36

Lesson #41: Other Ideas for Liberty

Let's try some different ideas — "fiddly-diddlies" — for LIBERTY. You can pick and choose the ones you like and want to learn to play now. Store the other ideas for a later time when you feel ready to "grow into" them.

First, let's consider our introduction. I like to have my intros *near* the location where I play the tune. In our simplified arrangement, we play on the open D and A strings (the middle register), and then we hop *up* to the E and A strings (upper register) to play the tune. While this is OK, I prefer my intro to also be *high* like the tune.

In Ex. 1, you could get along by playing this:

However, as I explained earlier, you want the *name of the key* (like the note D) present if you are *in* the key of D. Notice that the note D is *not* present in this intro chord. It doesn't quite sound complete to me, so these notes are not my favorite choice.

Ex. 2 contains my favorite choice. This is the *sound* I really like best! But it *is* more difficult to play because you have *two fingers* on two different strings at the same time (a double stop).

Try them all. Listen to your tape. You decide which one you like best and which suits your skill level at this time.

Doubling: Fiddlers will sometimes take *one note* and change it into *two notes*. I call this "doubling." You can use doubling in measure 1 and measure 5.

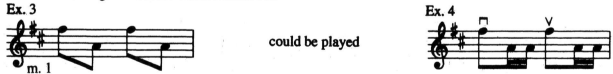

could be played

Double A's or *drone A's:* Measures 9, 11, and 13 are perfect spots to use your double A's. I just *love* this sound. To me it is the essence of fiddling. Have you noticed on how many tunes so far we have had the chance to use this technique? It really is tricky at first — it was for me, too — but, if you really *love* this wonderful sound, you'll be willing to work on it. It takes time, but it *is worth* the effort!

Did you remember to *slide* into the double A?

A more common way that fiddlers might play measure 15 would be as in Ex. 6. It is a little harder because it is a more complicated fingering. Practice this lick several times a day until you feel that it is easy for you. It occurs in many fiddle tunes!

The trick here is to remember to play *low 2 on* the E string and *high 2* on the A string.

Why? Because you are in the key of D.

Using these ideas plus the addition of our slides, alternate bowing pattern, and a double stop or two, here's a version of the way I like to play LIBERTY:

Lesson #42: Liberty (More Complicated Arrangement)
Arrangement #2

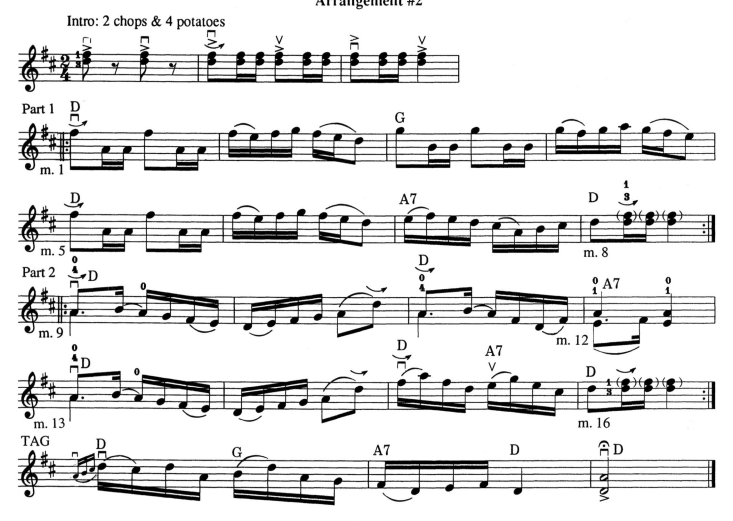

In measures 8 and 16, notice the note F# in parentheses. This is the double stop I personally like to play. If it's too hard for you at this time, it's OK to leave it out for now.

Generally speaking, most fiddle tunes are in two parts. Sometimes each part is repeated; in other tunes, you play them just once. In the above arrangement of LIBERTY, the shortest I would play it would be Part 1 (repeat), Part 2, Part 1 + Tag.

Lesson #43: Red Fox Waltz

Many tunes might be played more in certain areas than others. For example, the closer you are to Canada, the more you might hear the Canadian influence (like jigs and Canadian tunes). On the other hand, down in Texas you wouldn't hear too many jigs. Through modern technology such as tapes, records, and ease of traveling, there are exceptions. RED FOX WALTZ is a great old-time waltz that I have heard fiddlers from a variety of areas play. Again, this is one of those waltzes that I think sounds good either with a slower lyrical interpretation or a more perky, danceable tempo. Try it both ways! Remember that the more danceable you want to make it, the more of a fat 1 (emphasis on the first beat of the measure) you will want.

First, play RED FOX with just the basic melody.

Red Fox Waltz (Basic Tune)
Arrangement #1

Lesson #44: Red Fox Waltz with Ornaments

Before looking at my arrangement below, just for fun and a challenge, try RED FOX *by yourself* to see what ideas for decorations you can remember and come up with on your own. No peeking!

Now, together let's add some ornaments. Here's one more ornament for your collection, a *double slide*. This is one of my favorites, and I like it in measure 9.

To play this ornament, play the note *ever so briefly, slide down* out of it (only for a split second), then *slide up* and hang on the note. *Listen to your cassette tape and play along with me.* Notice the double arrows (⤵⤴), one pointing *down* and one pointing *up*.

Ex. 1

Red Fox Waltz with Ornaments & Tag
Arrangement #2

40

Lesson #45: Possible Endings for Red Fox Waltz

The style or mood I am trying to create helps determine what kind of an *ending tag* I use on my waltzes.

Long notes: Sometimes it just seems to fit the waltz to keep it simple and have a long note such as in our basic-tune example of RED FOX. I *always* plan my bowing to work out with this last note on a *down bow* (⊓). That way I am working with Mother Nature! The frog of the bow is heavier (and therefore *louder*), and a natural gradual softening (decrescendo) happens as I move my bow to the tip. Then I like to *hold it there* for a second or two. (Don't move and break the spell!) The audience will continue to think they hear you fading out. It's a very tasty effect and a neat trick to use.

If I want a lyrical style, I put on some kind of tag...usually some kind of arpeggio, but it doesn't necessarily have to be an arpeggio. Many ideas are possible, such as:

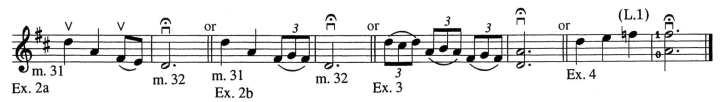

I think it is very important to kind of "wind down"...by slowing down (ritard) that last couple of measures.

If I want a more old-timey effect, I don't slow down, but do what I call "cha cha cha!," like this:

> Ending tags can be your chance for a personal touch if you choose, kind of like your personal signature. But remember: The secret is *not* so much *what* you choose to play, *but how you play it* (whether you play it well)!
>
> You could use any of the above endings for RED FOX or for any waltz in D.

Lesson #46: Rubber Dolly

Here's an old tune called RUBBER DOLLY that can be used as a tune of choice (a two-step) in a fiddle contest or for dancing. Some of the words to this old song go:

My mommy told me...
If I be goodie...
That she would buy me...
A rubber dolly...
So don't you tell her...
I've got a feller...
Or she won't buy me...
A rubber dolly...

41

Let's try just the notes of the basic melody. If you were to play this tune with all single bowing (one note = one bow), it could sound pretty choppy. Fiddlers use *slurs* (more than *one note* in one bow) to *smooth out* their fiddling. The slurring I use here helps smooth out the tune and also works the bowing so that you have a lot of *down bows* at the *down beat* (the first beat of the measure). If you need to, it's all right when learning the notes to leave out the slurs at first. But as soon as you feel ready, put them in so that they become a habit.

Rubber Dolly (Two-Step Basic Tune)
Arrangement #1

Once you feel comfortable with the notes, you can begin to "fiddle" RUBBER DOLLY by using the same techniques you used for TWINKLE and RHODY. You could start by adding a few slides (curved arrows).

The whole tune can be played on sets of double strings. This will give it a very full sound. You don't need to look at the music to play it on double strings. Just let the bow play *also* on the open E string whenever you are playing on the A string, and let the bow rub also on the A string when you are playing on the D string. This is what the music looks like when you write in all those open drone strings. Don't let it scare you. Now that you understand *how* to add the double strings, you know it is easier than it looks!

Lesson #47: Rubber Dolly with Double Strings
Arrangement #2

Measure 5 and measure 13 are great spots to use your double E's. Of course, playing your fourth finger on the A string while *also* playing the open E string *is* more difficult and more work, but it's worth it! It's such a great fiddle sound, especially when you slide into it.

Ex. 1. Optional variation for measures 5 and 13.

m. 5 or m. 13

Now here's a real challenge — *strictly for advanced fiddlers*. At measure 13, when you are ready to end the tune, you can give it a real feeling of finality by adding a *high second finger* on the E string (G♯) *while you also play* the *fourth finger on the A string* (the note E). If you do not feel like learning this advanced skill yet, it's OK to save it for later, but continue listening to your tape for this special fiddle sound. Probably someday you will love it so much you will be willing to put in the extra work to learn this skill.

Ex. 2. Optional advanced skill for measure 13.

Variations are ways to change something to make it different. Imagine chocolate-chip cookies. To change them to give them some variety, you could add nuts, raisins, or coconut. Here are more variations to RUBBER DOLLY. As you listen to your tape, you can decide which variation you really like and want to learn. Of course, it would be good to learn them all because you could use all of these ideas (variations) in other tunes, also!

Variation:"Doubling" is a nickname I made up for taking *one note* and making it into *two notes*. You will find doubling a very useful technique that you can use in almost every tune. In Arrangement #3 of RUBBER DOLLY, we will use it *seven* times (in the pick-up, then in measures 2, 4, 8, 10, 12, and 14).

Lesson #48: Rubber Dolly with Doubling
Arrangement #3

m. 1

m. 5

m. 11   m. 15   m. 16

Lesson #49: Bow Bobble

Variation: "Bow bobble" — a nickname I made up when I "bobble" my bow back and forth between two strings or two pairs of strings. It's very similar to our shuffle bowing we first learned in TWINKLE, but I call it "bobbing" because you are *changing* strings now instead of just staying on one string.

I find it really helps to think of my strings in *pairs:* top pair (E and A strings), middle pair (D and A), and bottom pair (G and D).

Now the tune starts to have a lot of activity. The written music also has a lot more notes, but listen to your tape, and *take your time!* You *can* do it! Play S-L-O-W-L-Y at first, then as your fingers and bow arm start to feel more comfortable, speed will come. I have been teaching a long time, and I have found that most people need to repeat a tune *at least* ten times per day for many days or weeks before they start to feel comfortable with it. The more you play it, the *sooner* speed comes!

Without using our fingers, let's practice the bow bobble (Ex. 1) with just pairs of open strings. When you feel comfortable, move your eyes from your strings down to your right wrist. Think: "Use your *wrist to change strings...not* your whole arm."

Ex. 1

Now that you can do bow bobbing, let's try using it in RUBBER DOLLY!

Rubber Dolly with Bow Bobble
Arrangement #4

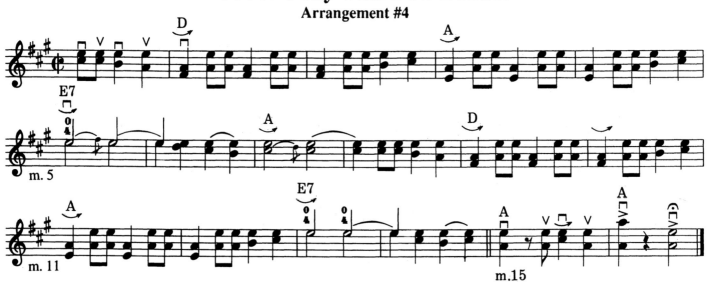

Lesson #50: Possible Endings for Rubber Dolly

Endings: Did you notice the new variation in the ending? Remember that endings are another chance for fiddlers to add their own personal touch. Here are a few more possibilities. Which ones do you like? Can you make up some endings of your own?

Ending #1. I like going down into the basement to end with the fat-finger technique.

Opt. ending   #1

44

Ending #2.
RUBBER DOLLY is in the key of A. You can use an A scale to make an ending.

Ending #3. You may wish to make the last note a long one.

To Ending #3. A completely different feel is given when you make the last notes very *short* and perky.

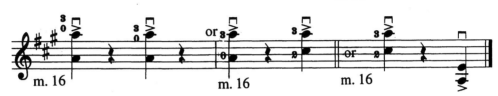

Ending #3 with a short last note.

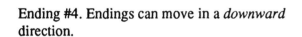

Ending #4. Endings can move in a *downward* direction.

Ending #5. Here's a kind of swingy little ending.

You can get more variety by simply changing one note.

> REMEMBER: It is not necessary to learn all of the endings. They are here to show you some of the ways that endings can have variety.

Lesson #51: Additional Ideas for Rubber Dolly

We have really had fun exploring different variations in RUBBER DOLLY, but before we leave this tune let's try just a couple more ideas that are fun to fiddle!

First try this "turnaround" for another way to play the pick-up notes at the beginning.

Ex. 1

45

Now add the drone open E string.

We are going to give RUBBER DOLLY a Cajun sound, so practice this little exercise. Be sure to use a *low* second finger to play the *first* F♮, and then *slide it up* to a *high 2*. And then use a *low 1* to make an E♭ and *slide it back up* to a regular 1 for E♮.

Great! Now just two more little steps and you'll be ready for a really neat arrangement with a Cajun flavor. First, add your open-A drone string.

In Louisiana the Cajun fiddlers give a spunky little accent on the off beat, so give a little "kick" to those notes with the accent (>) marks. Listen for this little kick on your tape.

I like to use a *high first* finger for the second and third F♯'s. It gives a cleaner sound.

Lesson #52: Rubber Dolly with a Cajun Beat
Arrangement #5

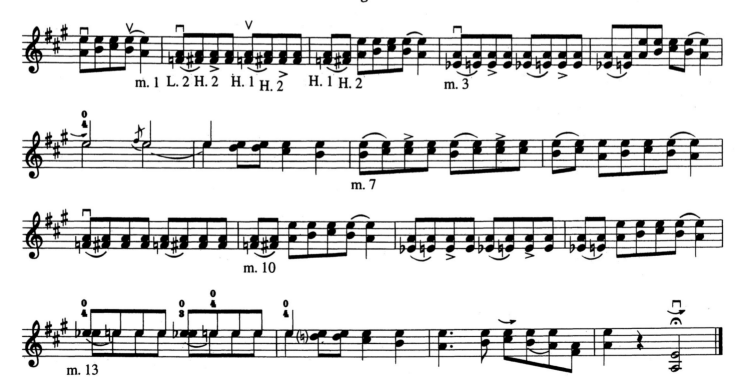

Here's a strictly *advanced* lick for measure 13. *While you are holding down* your fourth finger on the A string (the note E), also add your high *second finger* on the note G♯ on the E string. It is kind of tricky, but I really like the sound. If you do too, you'll want to work hard to acquire this skill.

Lesson #53: The Key of C

Through years of watching and listening to fiddlers, I have noticed that they often have some problems in the *key of C*. The reason for this is that they get used to playing in the keys of G, D, and A, where you use a *regular 1* (regular *first* finger) on the E string. In the key of C, it is *very important to use a low 1*. Also, on the D and A strings you will use a *low 2* when in the key of C (instead of *high 2*). The reason is this: The key of C has *no sharps and no flats*. Please memorize this and remember the information for other tunes in the key of C.

Let's review our finger patterns in the key of C by playing through the C scale in two octaves (two scales, one on top of the other).

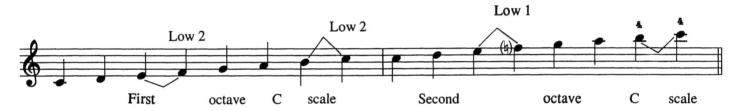

Remember that a scale always starts and *ends on the name of the key*. We start the C scale on the note C and end on the note C. Did you notice that you have to use *extension position* to play the last note? This means that after you play the note B with the fourth finger on the E string, you *stretch* your fourth finger *a half step higher*, about ½ inch, to make the last note C. If you have trouble reaching this note, be sure to pull your left elbow under the fiddle, and don't have your *left* thumb too high. Both of these tricks will give you a "longer" fourth finger!

⋀ or ⋁: These kinds of marks mean that the fingers are *close together* (because that is where the half steps fall in the scale). Don't let the key of C worry you. It's no big deal — just a matter of getting used to it — but *remember that low 1* on the E string.

Lesson #54: The Cowboy Waltz (Chromatic Finger Pattern)

Let's learn a waltz in the key of C called THE COWBOY WALTZ. I have also heard it called THE BLACK VELVET WALTZ. (A tune may have several names in the fiddling world.) This waltz comes from Canada, and I learned it many years ago from a fine fiddler, Bill Yohey (1919–1991), one of the founding fathers of the Oregon Old Time Fiddle Association. Bill was known for having a big, beautiful tone, which is important when you play this waltz in lyrical style. This waltz can also be played in a more up-tempo, old-timey, danceable style.

First let's get comfortable with the basic melody of the waltz. Notice in *Part 2* that you use both a *high* and *low* 1 on the E string.

Let's make an exercise out of this finger pattern so it won't give us any problems when we come to it in the tune.

This type of finger pattern is called a *"chromatic."* The word "chromatic" means to move by half steps, and that is what this finger pattern does. This happens a lot in fiddling.

Lesson #55: The Cowboy Waltz (Basic Tune)
Arrangement #1

SPECIAL TIP: Be very careful at measures 14 and 30 to play a *low* 1 on the E string (for the note F), then bring your first finger back to a *regular placement* on the A string (for the note B).

Lesson #56: The Cowboy Waltz (Fiddle Style)

Using many of the ideas we have already learned is one way you could "fiddle" THE COWBOY WALTZ. Remember you do *not* have to play it exactly as I do. It's OK to play only those ornaments you feel you can handle at this time. You can come back later and *add* more ornaments as you feel ready to grow into them.

The Cowboy Waltz with Ornaments
Arrangement #2

What does the key of C mean to you as a fiddler?

Answer: A *low 1* on the E string, *low 2's* on the E, A, and D strings, and *no* high 3's anywhere.

49

Lesson #57: Preparing for Boil the Cabbage

We have already worked on the A scale one octave. Now let's play it in *two* octaves. Remember that the slanted lines (∧) indicate where the half steps are.

As a fiddler, you need to memorize what the key of A means to you: a *high* third finger on the G and D strings, but a *regular* third finger on the A and E strings. The second finger is *high* on *all* strings.

After you feel comfortable with the A scale playing single notes (one note = one bow), then click into the alternate bowing pattern.

There is a lot of shuffle bowing (hoedown rhythm = long, short, short) in BOIL THE CABBAGE. In the Part 2 variation, change strings as you do the shuffle bowing. Be sure to use your *wrist* to change strings and not your whole arm.

Here's a little exercise to practice using your wrist:

Actually turn your head and *look* down at your wrist. Send the message down your bow arm: "Wrist, relax! Wrist, relax!"

Now do the same exercise on *two* strings. When you are on the D string, let the A string sound. When you are on the A string, let the E string sound.

Look in a mirror at your wrist. Does it *feel* relaxed? Does it *look* relaxed?

Lesson #58: Boil the Cabbage (Hoedown)

I have played BOIL THE CABBAGE for over 17 years and still love it. I have passed this tune on to hundreds of fiddlers. It can be played by the very young (4- and 5-year olds) through any age, and audiences love it. You can stay with the basic tune or get fancy with "hokum" bowing and left-hand pizzicato. At many of my workshops we even learn how to play it with trick fiddling (fiddling behind your back or under your knee)!

I will show you many different ways to play BOIL THE CABBAGE. Learn as many as you can handle at this time, then grow into some of the other arrangements as you feel ready for them.

Boil the Cabbage (Simple Version)
Arrangement #1

Lesson #59: Boil the Cabbage (Third Part)

For most people, the part that gives them trouble is the *third* part. Knowing that, I gave you a pretty easy version to get you started.

Below is a version closer to the way I usually teach it. For our first project in "dressing up" BOIL THE CABBAGE, let's learn it.

Ex. 1

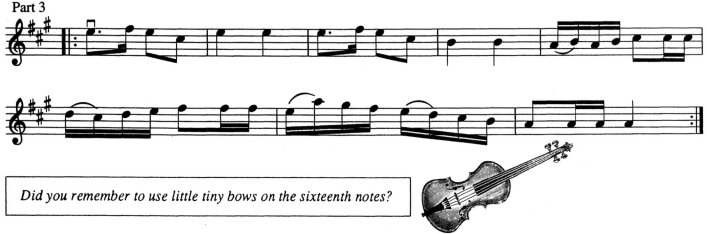

> *Did you remember to use little tiny bows on the sixteenth notes?*

Let's spend a little more time on the third part. I put some slurs in the above arrangement, and sometimes I *do* play it bowed as above. I also enjoy putting in more slurs, giving it an even smoother sound. I also enjoy "bending" the F♯ note with a slide.

In preparation for our next step in BOIL, I have also played it on *two* strings. Now this *looks* really complicated when you see it written out, but please don't worry…it is not that hard. Remember to play Ex. 1 and send the message to your arm: "Bow, play on *two* strings." Ex. 2 is what this looks like.

Ex. 2

Lesson #60: Boil the Cabbage with Double Strings

When you can play through the third part on double strings, then adding double strings to *all* of BOIL THE CABBAGE will be no problem. The music does look busy when written out, but remember to play the whole tune on the A and E strings, except when playing the second part. Part 2 is on the D string, so *let your bow also play on the A string here*.

We have recycled one of our old shaves, and look! In the last measure, see the "+" for one note of (left-hand) pizzicato! Fun!

Boil the Cabbage with Double Strings
Arrangement #2

Key of A

Lesson #61: Two-Finger Double Stop

Double stop in first part: In Arrangement #2 of BOIL THE CABBAGE, the entire tune is played with drone strings (when you are on the E string, let the A string drone, etc.). I like this sound, with the exception of measures 2 and 6. I don't really care for the D note against the open E string. It's a fine way to get started playing on two strings in BOIL, but as soon as you can handle it, make your very first goal to learn this *real double stop*. I call it "real" because it involves *two* fingers on two strings.

Ex. 1. This is what is written in measures 2 and 6.

m. 2 & m. 6

Ex. 2. This is the *double stop* I like to play for measures 2 and 6.

m. 2 & m. 6

Now, if you decide to play this double stop, it is *most important* that it is *in tune*. It sounds terrible when it is not!

It helps me to play this little exercise in *three steps*. It helps my fingers *memorize* how this double stop *feels*...as well as *how it sounds*. Practice it S-L-O-W-L-Y first, and when you feel it is *in tune*, begin to play it faster.

Ex. 3. Double-stop exercise.

Practice on one string, then the other, then *together!*

When I teach this double stop, I remind students to keep a "close action" (keep your fingers close to the fingerboard — don't let them fly into the air several inches above it).

Also *very important* to keeping in tune: When you transfer your first finger over to the E string, make sure it goes *straight* across the fingerboard from B to F♯...this will help you play it in tune. These two notes are *right next door to each other*.

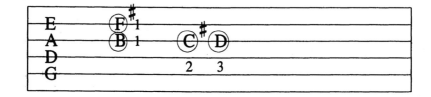

Lesson #62: Boil the Cabbage (Optional Variations)
For Part 1 — The Turnaround

Form: Did you notice that the form (shape) we used in Arrangement #2 was: first part (repeat), second part (repeat), first part (repeat), third part (repeat)? This would be a fine arrangement. However, I usually like to return to the first part again at the end. When I do, I give a little "yelp!" or call out "Hit it!" and then everyone plays it fast. Of course, you really have to have the first part down well to do this.

In Arrangement #2, *all* the first parts are *the same*. And that's fine for now, but someday you may choose to play different variations of the first part (as I do).

When you feel ready, here are some to try:

I call Ex. 1 the "turnaround variation" because it has a little finger pattern that many fiddlers call a "turnaround," I guess because they make a little turn-around pattern if you use your imagination.

see: →

Let's play it first just on *one* string:

The Turnaround Variation

Ex. 1 on *one* string.

Now try the *same* thing on *two* strings. Notice that, except for measure 7 where you go onto the D string for two quick sixteenth notes, the whole part is played with the E string droning.

The Turnaround Variation on Two Strings

Ex. 2 on *two* strings.

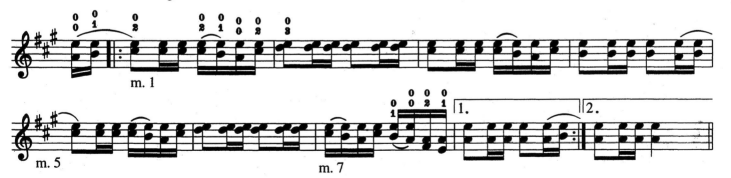

Now, are you feeling brave?! Want to try it with the *real* double stop? It will probably feel very awkward at first, but the more you play it, the easier it will be for your fingers. Soon they will *feel* comfortable going to this double stop. It is a *very* useful combination used in countless tunes. Make a vow to work on it for one week. I'll bet you'll see some improvement! Then, at the end of a month's time, it will really be easy for you!

Here's Ex. 1 written out with the *real double stops:*

Turnaround Variation on Two Strings with Real Double Stops

Lesson #63: The Pizzicato Variation

Here's a really fun one! I just love this *pizzicato* variation! It's terrific for jams, shows, and entertaining.

The "+" means *left-hand* pizzicato. The number indicates *which finger* you pluck with. Since you have just played with your second finger, it works just fine this time to pluck with it. Confidently *pull* your second finger off the A and E strings at the same time…make them "snap" — make the notes seem to "pop out"!

Here's a little *left-hand pizzicato exercise* to help prepare us for this fun variation:

Get a real "swing" of the bow arm going. As you play, think, "Bow! Pluck! Bow! Pluck!" with one bow stroke *down* and the next bow stroke *up*.

Or you might prefer to think, "*Down,* pluck! *Up,* pluck!," etc.

Now we'll put the *left-hand* pizzicato into the first part (Ex. 2) on *one* string only.

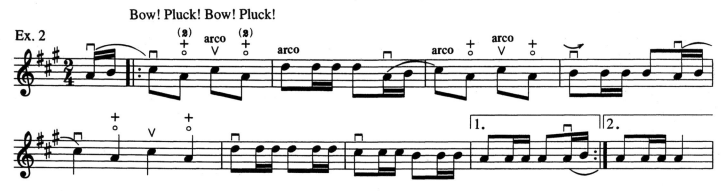

Then on *two strings:*

Finally, when you feel ready to take on the ultimate challenge, the *pizzicato* variation on *two strings with the real double stops:*

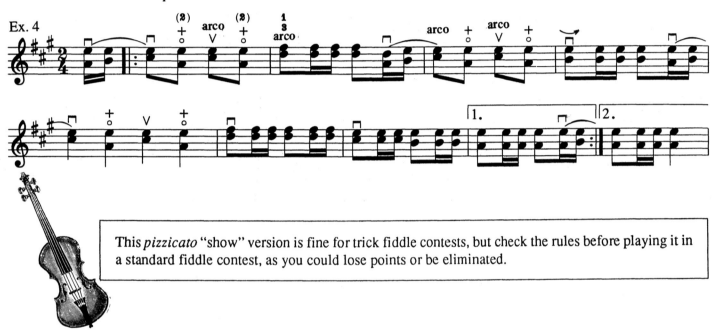

This *pizzicato* "show" version is fine for trick fiddle contests, but check the rules before playing it in a standard fiddle contest, as you could lose points or be eliminated.

Lesson #64: Boil the Cabbage (Putting It All Together!)

Fiddling can be creative. Now that we have explored several different ways to play BOIL THE CABBAGE, let's combine some of them.

Using the ideas we have learned so far, here's one possible arrangement. If you are not yet playing all of these parts, it's OK — you can add them later. Just substitute any you feel comfortable with. You can even play the *same* first part over and over, then "hit it" (play it as fast as you can) the last time through the first part. The audience will still enjoy it.

PERFORMING TIP: One secret of playing in front of an audience is to look like you are having a good time. So, when you announce your tune, *smile!* And at the end, when the audience claps for your fiddling, acknowledge them, give a little "thank you!" and *smile* again!

Form for Arrangement #3:

Introduction
Part 1   (repeat)
Part 2   (repeat with doubling or shuffle bowing)
Part 1   turnaround variation
                (on repeat, *pizzicato* variation)
Part 3   regular way (my favorite)
                (repeat, the same)
Return to Part 1   play it fast if you can!
                (repeat)
Ending tag   double shave

Here's what the music *looks* like. Listen to your tape to hear what it *sounds* like. And *please*, remember this is just one possible arrangement. If there are some parts that you do not feel ready for, you can substitute other parts. I have played Part 1 here *three* different ways, but you could play them all the same.

> GREAT LEARNING TIP: Listen with *earphones* to BOIL THE CABBAGE several times in bed just before sleep. Then while you sleep, your subconscious will continue working and learning!

Boil the Cabbage
Arrangement #3

59

Lesson #65: Silver Bell

SILVER BELL is a two-step that is over 80 years old. My son used to play this tune when he was about 8, 9, and 10 years old. Originally it was called SILVER BELL (INDIAN INTERMEZZO). An "intermezzo" is something that goes in between, so this was played in the middle of old-time movies before sound. It has also been played by fiddlers as a two-step for dancing. On the cover of a copy of the original music, it has a lovely picture of a Native American couple. Indians supplied the inspiration for many old American fiddle tunes like SNOW DEER, RED WING, LOST INDIAN, etc.

In Arrangement #1 you will hear the way my son and I play SILVER BELL. I thought you might also enjoy hearing and seeing the melody of the first part from the old original (see Ex. 1) as it used to be played on piano in those old movie houses long ago. Arrangement #1 shows you how fiddlers take a tune and "fiddle" it. If you wish, you may substitute Ex. 1 for the first part in our arrangement or *add* it to our arrangement, creating a new one. It is very common for fiddlers to add their own special little touch or personality to their tunes. We like to play this two-step with a kind of bouncy feeling. This also gives the tune danceability.

Silver Bell (Indian Intermezzo)

Percy Wenrich
1910

Lesson #66: Silver Bell (Two-Step Basic Tune)

In Arrangement #1 we have the *notes* of the basic tune the way I play it.

In Arrangement #2 we have the tune with a couple of variations, some slides, and lots of ornaments added. Don't feel that you *have* to play every single ornament as I have written here. In fact it's quite common for fiddlers *not* to do every single ornament and "noodlely-noodlely" every single time they play the tune. Do as many ornaments as you feel you can handle at this time.

Ex. 1

L. 2 H. 2

About bowing: The opening notes occur several times in SILVER BELL. My personal way of bowing it involves a *down* bow, followed by two *up* bows. I call this a "hooked bow" (you hook two notes together). This bowing feels good to me, as does the rest of the bowing in this tune. It also helps set me up for a *down bow* on the *down beat* when the tune begins.

When I can, *generally speaking,* I like to use a *down bow on the down beat.* This does not always happen, however. I just don't worry about it.

Did you notice the *chromatic* notes at the beginning? These and others happen several times in SILVER BELL.

> *If you like a certain fiddler's style or arrangement, learning the notes is only 50%. You also need to listen very carefully and copy,* as closely as possible, *the bowing in order to really capture the sound.*

I have marked the bowing as I play it. There are many other ways to bow this tune that are just as correct as mine. Feel free to change it, but remember:

> *To capture a fiddler's sound, capture the bowing!*

61

Silver Bell (Two-Step Basic Tune)
Arrangement #1

Key of G

by Percy Wenrich 1910

Lesson #67: Silver Bell (Two-Step) with Ornaments
Arrangement #2

Lesson #68: McNabs Hornpipe

Different styles of fiddling: Just as people from different states or countries have different accents, different ways they dress, or different flavors in their foods, the same will be true of their fiddling. It will have different sounds (styles) or accents. There are *so many* things that I love about fiddle, but surely the *fact that it can have so many different sounds* is my favorite!

Here we will try a Canadian-style tune, McNABS HORNPIPE. Most Canadian tunes have a very happy, perky sound to them. They use fewer double stops, have a more choppy style, and the fast tunes are lively!

I have played McNABS HORNPIPE for so many years, I don't even remember who I learned it from. There is a Scottish tune called CROSSING THE MINCH that sounds very much like it, so it may have Scottish roots.

This particular arrangement is a Canadian-style arrangement. McNABS was one of the tunes played by my daughter Tiffany in 1982 when she won the National Junior Junior Fiddle Championship. It was one of her favorite contest tunes. It was not necessarily the *tune* that helped her win, but it was the way she played it...*clean, clear, solid, with good tone.*

Remember the *important thing* in a good performance or in playing in a fiddle contest:

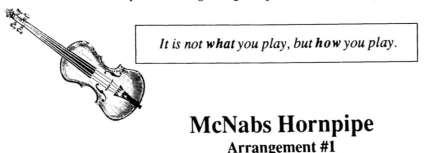

> *It is not **what** you play, but **how** you play.*

McNabs Hornpipe
Arrangement #1

For the most part, the hoedown rhythm (shuffle bowing) used at the beginning of tunes is an American characteristic. For example, you won't find it in Irish, Scottish, or Swedish styles of fiddling. Two quick chops will be fine for an introduction to McNABS. The first note (F♯) in measure 1 is your travel note.

Key of D
Intro: 2 chops

64

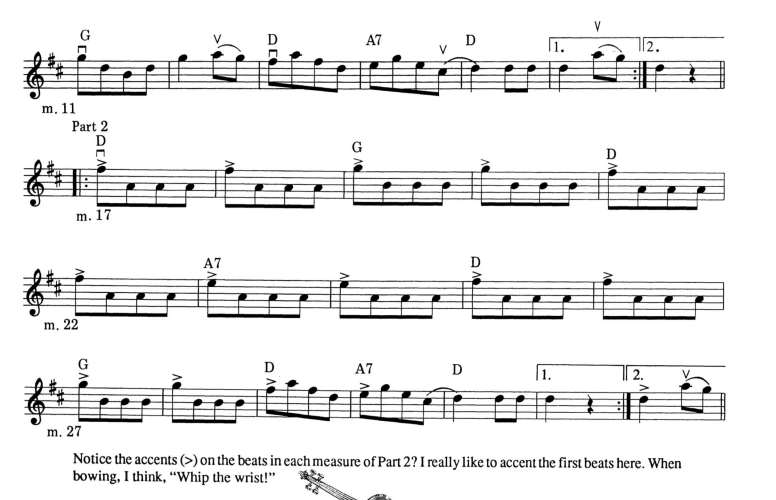

Notice the accents (>) on the beats in each measure of Part 2? I really like to accent the first beats here. When bowing, I think, "Whip the wrist!"

> *Use a mirror to watch your flexible wrist.*

Lesson #69: Bowing Variation for McNabs Hornpipe

Often in this book I mention how important *bowing* is in fiddling. You'll see now how changing the bowing *only* in a tune can change the whole sound of the tune!

Here's a variation for the second part. You could bow it with all separate bows, but I really like the style of bowing where you have one note *alone* and then *three notes* slurred *together*. If you use this bowing, you will need to whip your wrist more than ever! What is actually happening is that you use *the same amount of bow for the three slurred notes that you use for the one note alone.*

My personal favorite is to play the second part first (as in Lesson #68) with single noting, then on a repeat play this variation:

2nd Part - variation

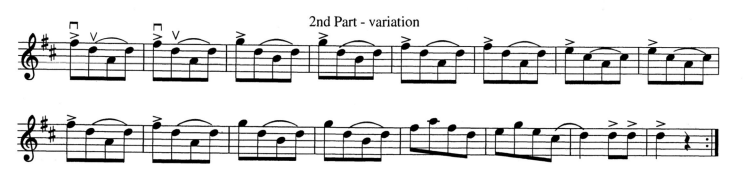

Lesson #70: Hokum Bowing

Hokum bowing (also called "double shuffle"): The term "hokum bowing" refers to a special style of bowing. It is usually considered to be fancy or trick bowing, and it is kind of tricky to learn but worth the work!

Hokum bowing involves uneven groups of notes (especially *two notes* on one string and *one note* on the other string). *Accenting* is very *important* to making the correct sound.

Let's use open strings to learn one basic pattern of hokum. Notice that the accents in this pattern happen on the *upper string* and that one time it is a *down* bow and the next time an *up* bow.

In the beginning, your brain will direct your bowing...as you think, "Down!...Up!...Down!...Up!" But it is important that you play the musical example so much that *you do not have to use your brain to think...*you simply *hear* it in your ear and *feel* it in your heart. Play slowly and build speed over a period of time.

Play the example on your other two pairs of strings. It would be best if you *did not* try using your fingers in hokum bowing until you have conquered the open strings. This might take some time. I am embarrassed how long it took me to learn hokum, but in those days no one could play it slowly for me like I will for you. It's a great sound! And you will find lots of tunes that you can use it in.

Lesson #71: McNabs Hornpipe with Hokum Bowing

> Use *small bows* and your *wrist* (not your bowing arm) when changing strings in hokum bowing.

Now, just for fun and when you want a challenge, here's the second part again, this time using a hokum-bowing variation. *Do not* use this variation or hokum bowing in standard fiddle contests. It is considered trick fiddling, and there is the possibility you could be eliminated or penalized for playing it. It is a fun bowing to do for shows and entertainment, however.

2nd part-Hokum bowing variation

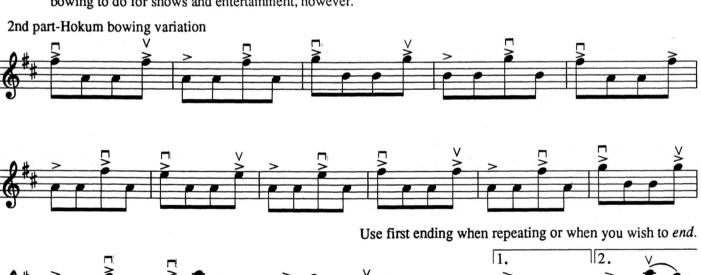

Use first ending when repeating or when you wish to *end*.

Use second ending when returning to the first part.

We now have *three* different ways to play the second part. Let's combine all of our parts to make one of my favorite arrangements (Arrangement #2) of McNABS. What a fun tune to play! And the more you play it, the faster it gets.

Lesson #72: McNabs Hornpipe
Arrangement #2

Key of D
Intro: 2 chops

Lesson #73: Endings

We have explored lots of old-time traditional fiddle endings. I like to have my endings "fit" or "go with" the style of the tune. Our "Shave and a Haircut" ending is pretty much an American style, and personally I don't care to use it on my Canadian tunes.

Ending McNABS: You can end McNABS after the first part or after the second part. My favorite choice is to save the hokum for the end of the tune, then come to a *really abrupt,* crisp, bold stop on that last D note. Very simple, yet quite effective when performed well. You'll want to warn your back-up about this ending. *Look* at them. Frequently, fiddlers will lift one leg (their hands and arms are too busy!) to signal, "Hey, here we come to the end." But for this particular ending, I think that a special look or nod is good body language to remind them, "Watch out, something different is happening!" Listen to this ending on your tape and see how you like it.

Ex. 1. Get *right off this last note.* Tell your back-up to watch you here and get off this note, also.

And speaking of endings! This is the end of this volume. I congratulate you on sticking with me to the end. I look forward to sharing lots of new *old* fiddle tunes as you continue to learn about the *wonderful world of fiddling!*

Most sincerely,

Carol Ann

Great Music at Your Fingertips